Table of Contents

Introduction: The Power of Effective Communication

Communicating is something we take for granted. We do every day, and people pay attention to us when we are having a conversation. As a result, it seems like a pretty natural process that doesn't require preparation. Unfortunately, it's a common fallacy to have this mindset about professional presentation. Underestimating professional communication by likening it to "just talking" will waste the audience's time; they will unlikely retain all of the key points, and may lose interest in the presentation altogether.

In an academic setting, communication skills are underestimated, also. When starting a communication course, students often question the value of spending 3 hours a week learning how to "just talk." By the end of the course, though, those students have received invaluable skills that can be applied across any industry, especially as a future leader. Regardless of where you end up as a leader, chances are you will need to communicate your ideas and convince and inspire others towards a certain goal.

This book is designed to transform you into that effective communicator by giving you the right ideas and strategies to tune your presentation and professional communication. I assume you want to improve your professional communication in some way, which is why you decided to read this book. This may come in the form of sales pitches, internal meetings, conference presentations, or interviews.

The strategies presented in this book are not ground-breaking secrets. In fact, many of the lessons and suggestions may seem obvious after reading them, but the problem is, most people have not considered how to actively and effectively apply them. Most often, these strategies are used haphazardly, and it becomes a hit-or-miss in terms of their effectiveness. This book not only lists out the strategies but also explains why they are useful, when to use them, and how to use them. By actively managing them, you will have more consistent outcomes with your presentations.

The Foundations examines various ideas that a presenter should understand. These ideas are focused primarily on the audience and how they think or feel throughout a presentation. After learning these ideas, you will be able to use communication strategies more purposefully because you will know why you are using them.

The Strategy provides various frameworks I've designed to help guide you in crafting your presentation. It takes the ideas and lessons from the Foundations section, and transcribes them into actions that produce the desired effect on your audience.

The Execution focuses on fine-tuning your presentation through planning and review. At this stage of the book, you should be ready to craft your message. The first guide I have provided in this section serves as an outline of key points to consider as you craft the presentation. The second guide is a tool to help you review your own presentation as you practice, and quickly identify areas for improvement.

How to Effectively Use This Book

While this book covers strategies for a professional presentation, the strategies that are discussed can be carried to other aspects of professional and personal communication. I encourage you to use what you learn in this book when speaking with colleagues or managers because, at the very least, it gives you more practice for professional presentations. Practice not only makes perfect--it also builds habit.

Before reading the rest of this book , I recommend you record yourself presenting. This is a benchmark for you, as a way to see where you are. Then, this book will act as a guide to help bring your current presentation skills to the next level.

First, set a baseline. To do this, you should design a 3-5 minute presentation. You can think of a question to answer, or if you don't want to, here's a prompt for you: "What is something fascinating to you, and why should it be fascinating for us as well?"

After you design the presentation, record yourself presenting it. Then set it aside and go through the rest of this book. Don't immediately review your recording because you might not be entirely sure what to look for. Also, you want to give yourself some time to forget about your presentation--this will act like a palette cleanser, and it will give you a fresher lens to examine it. When you do come back to your presentation after reading the book, you'll be able to find clear areas of improvement based on what you've learned.

Therefore, after learning the strategies in this book, watch your recording again. Through the guidance of my communications professor, I have learned that the most thorough way of reviewing your own recorded presentation is to do it three times:

1. In the first review, only listen to your voice (don't watch anything).
2. In the second review, only watch the video (mute it).
3. Finally, in the third review, watch the recording with audio.

As an added bonus, you should find someone who can review your first video alongside yourself. Both of you should have a copy of the rubric; after watching the video, compare notes and check to see if you have the same perception of the various aspects of the presentation. Chances are, your perceptions will be slightly different because every audience member receives information in a different manner, but the good thing about doing this is that getting another perspective will help you identify other areas for improvement.

As you (and maybe your partner as well) review each time, take notes on what could be improved. In *The Execution* section of the book, I have created a Presentation Planner and a Presentation Reviewer, based on everything this book will teach you. The Presentation Planner should be used beforehand as a guide to help you prepare your presentation; the Presentation Reviewer should be used after you record your practice, as a guide to help you (or another listener) identify strengths and areas of improvement that you can then use to iterate and improve your presentation.

Finally, redo your presentation based on your notes for improvement. Review your new presentation from the lens of an audience member. You'll notice strategies like repeating yourself may seem silly at first but sound quite natural and effectively reinforce your message.

In summary, I've outlined below the steps that you should take to use this book in the most effective manner possible:

1. Create a 5-minute mock presentation before going through the rest of the book. If you can't think of a topic, you can use this one: "What is something fascinating to you, and why should it be fascinating for us as well?"
2. Record yourself giving the presentation.
3. Set the recording and your presentation aside.
4. Learn the strategies discussed in this book.
5. Review your recorded presentation using the Presentation Review Guideline found in the Execution section of the book. Take extensive notes: what you think you did well and what you think you can improve on.
6. Apply those ideas and do the same presentation over again, reconstructing whatever areas you think need adjustment.

7. Review the new presentation.

Throughout the book, you will also find exercises, labeled as *Try It Out*. These exercises are included to help you practice what you have learned. I encourage you to follow the instructions and try each of them. They will help you quickly identify areas of improvement by giving you a scenario where you can consciously focus on different aspects of your presentation style.

Myths of Presenting

To be a good presenter, you must think like a good presenter. To do this, you need to get used to habits you may find uncomfortable, such as repeating yourself. When I tell people to repeat themselves, they tend to nod their heads in agreement but don't follow through when presenting because they think it's redundant and may seem silly to the audience. In reality, not doing this is silly because it impacts the effectiveness of the message--how it is presented and how it sinks in with the audience. Common false assumptions that presenters often take to be true include:

1. I Just Need to Be Natural

There's a difference between being natural and acting natural. As a presenter, you want to act natural, not necessarily be natural. For example, stage fright is a natural reaction for many presenters on stage. Just because it's natural to start trembling doesn't mean it's effective for grabbing your audience's attention--at least, not in the way you want. The best way to act naturally is to prepare.

2. I Don't Have to Repeat Myself

Long story short, yes you do. In *The Foundations* section, I explain why repetition is a powerful and simple technique that can increase the likelihood that your audience will clearly understand and retain your message.

In *The Strategy* section, I will walk you through how to structure your presentation content. I use the acronym DRILS (I'll explain what each letter stands for in detail in the Strategy section), which is a reminder that you need to drill an idea into your audience's head. The R in DRILS stands for *Repeat, Repeat, Repeat.* Unlike in a normal conversation, presentation communication requires repetition because the engagement style is different.

3. I Don't Need to Practice

During my father's medical school talent show, the judges recited text from pages in a textbook, and my father would tell the audience which page and paragraph the text was from. He has what's called an eidetic memory (commonly known as a photographic memory). Regardless of this talent, he still spends hours studying and preparing. Despite all the acronyms you will memorize in this book, and all the strategies you will learn based on those acronyms, you will not be able to execute them without practicing. For example, you will need to remember to use certain words, where to place the right emphasis, where to take pauses, etc. Don't get me wrong, I'm not saying you have to memorize your presentation--but you need to be familiar with it to a point where all of the key strategies are mapped out, and you trigger them one by one to effectively get your point across to your audience.

4. *My Data Will Speak for Me*

"I used to believe that numbers did the work, and that if there was evidence that supported an argument and I could show it, then I was done with convincing my audience." That statement may sound familiar. I've heard it many times from many people. It accurately describes an assumption many presenters have: evidence is enough to persuade an audience. In a presentation, though, presenting evidence is only a piece of the entire process. A presenter must effectively control their audience's attention so that when the presenter explains the evidence, the audience will be listening and willing to absorb it.

Part 1: The Foundations

In this section, I want to lay the foundation that drives all of the persuasive communication strategies presented in this book. By doing this, you are not just understanding what to do (*The Strategy*), but why you do it (*The Foundations*). Many, if not all, of these theories are commonly practiced in various aspects of professional and personal life, but they have one thing in common: they all focus on the audience, not the presenter. Understanding the audience's emotions, habits, and expectations and being able to execute your presentation in a manner that aligns with those in some way will increase the audience's tendency to listen and agree.

The Audience Cannot Multitask

Your audience is either paying attention to you or they're not. Humans can only focus on one thing at a time. Christine Rosen, the Chair of the Colloquy on Knowledge, Technology & Culture at the Institute for Advanced Studies in Culture, dissects the realities of multitasking[1]. In her article, Christine offers various data points that speak to the limited potential of the human brain's ability to multitask. She references a study conducted by the Institute of Psychiatry, which refers to extraneous events that require attention as "distractions." A report of the findings published by the BBC stated that "those distracted by incoming email and phone calls saw a 10-point fall in their IQ - more than twice that found in studies of the impact of smoking marijuana[2]."

Multitasking is a dreamy illusion. At best, some people may feel more comfortable jumping between tasks than others. In those instances, attention is still given to one task at a time. In reality, a person's ability to effectively absorb information or work productively falls, and that drop is steep because of a lack of focus, which takes time and concentration.

When it comes to listening to your presentation, your audience's attention is either on you or it's not. They can be distracted with their own tools such as cell phones and laptops; they can be distracted mentally with daydreaming or thinking about other tasks; and they can be distracted by your presentation through poorly designed slides or confusing non-verbal expressions. While you can't control the audience's decision to focus on other tasks, you can minimize the likelihood of losing focus on you through the presentation strategies discussed in this book.

Each communication strategy decision you make does one of three things in regards to its impact on attention:

1. The audience pays more attention to you than previously
2. The audience continues to pay attention to you
3. The audience loses attention. For example, while adding as much information as possible on a slide can be informative for the audience, what you risk happening is that they will stop paying attention to you and focus on the content of the slides.

If it doesn't seem obvious, your decision on each strategy should lead the audience to do #1 or #2. While continuously doing #1 sounds ideal, it is tough because each time an audience increases attention, they are required to spend more mental energy. High mental energy for long periods of time is unsustainable in a passive-thinking environment like listening to a presentation; on the other hand, in active-thinking environments like an exam setting, it is more sustainable by doing things like adding curve-ball questions. But you're not giving your audience an exam, so don't expect constant increases in active attention. Think of it as a track and your audience are casual runners. If you motivate them, they may temporarily pick up speed, but eventually, they'll go back to a comfortable pace, especially if it's not a race.

Grab Their Attention

Because audience members cannot multitask, the presenter must fight for their attention against other activities such as checking phones, surfing the Internet on laptops, and falling asleep. The human attention span is short. Apps such as TikTok, Instagram, Facebook, and Reddit understand this so they give you short bursts of texts, videos, images, and other multimedia. Users quickly jump from one topic to another (e.g., from looking at a photo of a sleeping puppy to looking at a photo of a string cheese pizza). Conditioned through the consumption of information in this short-burst format, attention span has shortened. A 2004 study observed that exposing children to TV at an earlier age (yes, children watched TV in 2004) was associated with increased attention problems later on in life[3]. In 2015, Microsoft Canada published a report on the human attention span, stating that the average human was around 8 seconds in 2013[4]. That data doesn't bode well for an hour-long presentations.

Don't be too discouraged--depending on your definition of attention, audiences can provide more than 8 seconds. Generally, attention can be considered active or passive[5],[6]. Active attention is less likely to be sustainable, because it requires a high degree of mental effort. For example, memorizing a list of new vocabulary words needs focused attention. On the other hand, passive attention does not require high mental effort; for example, watching a television show does not require the viewer to actively pay attention to every detail in order to get the main idea and events of the episode.

In a presentation setting, audiences may start with active attention but will change to a state of passive attention as the presentation continues. That's part of what makes an introduction so important. While the introduction serves to "hook" an audience, it also gives the presenter an opportunity to take advantage of the active attention that the audience is offering. We will talk about how to do both later.

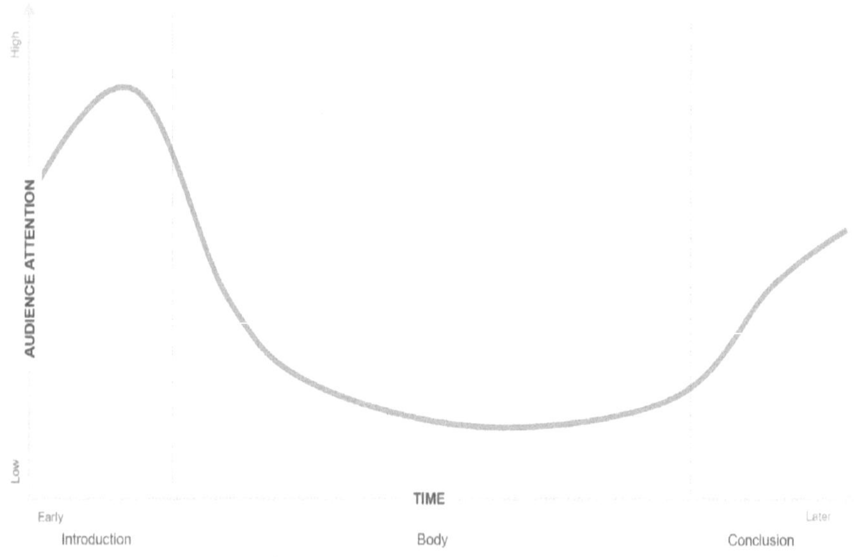

As the presentation progresses, an audience's attention drops. The graph above illustrates the overall attention that an average audience member gives to a presentation. As discussed recently, audience attention is highest during the introduction. At that point in time, the audience comes into the room with a high level of interest due to their expectation of the presentation. If their expectations do not align with the information they're receiving, then the audience will lose attention much more quickly. As the presenter goes into the body of the presentation, attention usually begins to wane. By the conclusion, the audience refocuses attention to try to capture any points they may have missed in the body (which also speaks to the importance of repeating); as a result, their attention increases again.[7]

What's In It for Them (WIIFT)

A good way to grab your audience's attention immediately is to think about what's in it for them, which is often referred to by the acronym WIIFT[8]. Chances are, the people sitting in the room listening to you weren't forced into the room against their will. They came to look for something, and it's your responsibility to give it to them; otherwise, they have little obligation to listen.

Aligning with what the audience wants and what you are delivering to them will enhance their experience with the presentation. By giving that positive experience, audiences are more inclined to listen and agree because they are getting a perspective or understanding that they came to learn. On the other hand, misaligning with the audience's expectations will push them in the other direction. They will stop paying attention because they believe they cannot get the relevant information; they may feel cheated because the title or description of the presentation gave them a different impression, which may have lured them into the presentation.

The latter has frequently happened to me during industry conferences. As an audience member, I am often inundated with various topics and talks happening simultaneously, each one sounding more interesting than the next. After committing to one, I get excited about learning. Upon sitting and listening for a few minutes, though, I realize that it quickly becomes a sales pitch, and I will not get educated on the topic. Instead, the education is around an understanding of a company-specific product, which misaligns with my expectations. Believing that this presentation can no longer deliver the value I was expecting, I quickly lose interest.

Align your messaging with the audience's expectations. Do not promise anything in a title or description that you will not deliver on honestly in the presentation. This means that if you are discussing trends in artificial intelligence, you should not be pitching your AI company as a trend in the space. To effectively incorporate your WIIFT, you should ask yourself why your audience is there in the first.

When a startup goes out to raise money from investors, one of the biggest mistakes I see is the lack of financial information or projections. The founder(s) may want to focus more on the story and the problem, but by not explaining their thought process on the financial viability of the business, they have most likely missed the WIIFT: an investment group is usually investing money on behalf of their clients, and their clients expect a return on that investment. As world-changing as the startup idea may be, it likely needs to include some discussion on financial return. By bringing up the discussion, the founders demonstrate that they understand the investment firm's needs. Showing this understanding increases the likelihood that the firm would want to work with them.

Repetition

In a 2016 publication of the *Journal of Experimental Social Psychology*, researchers Stefan Schulz-Hardt, Annika Giersiepen, and Andreas Mojzisch examined the effects of repetition as a tool for persuasion[9]. Because repetition is redundancy, they hypothesized repeating information should not affect or influence a listener's decision.

Their findings, though, suggested otherwise. In their two experiments outlined in the paper, they demonstrated that 1) repeating information in favor of a particular decision increased the listener's favor for that decision, and 2) increases the likelihood of the listener making a decision in favor of that decision. In other words, repetition is a powerful tool for persuasion.

The significance of repetition can be understood through the lens of learning. When learning, a person should consistently expose themselves to a new idea. The repeated exposure improves the brain's ability to both understand and retain the information. By repeating your messages to your audience, you are exposing them to it, which gives them the same opportunity to better understand and retain your main idea.

Presenters may find it uncomfortable to present information or say things repetitively at first. The redundancy feels unnecessary and presenters may think they are wasting their audience's time by doing so; as a result, they avoid it. Do not avoid it. Repetition is one of the easiest practices you can do to quickly improve the effectiveness of your presentations to your audience.

The Rule of Threes

Three is a magical number when it comes to communicating ideas. Instilled at a young age through stories like *The Three Little Pigs*, we have come to find the idea of three not only easier to remember but also a comfortable amount of substance that produces a complete and memorable story. This practice extends beyond storytelling. In physics, students learn about Newton's three laws of motion. In religion, followers learn about the story of the Three Wise Men and the Holy Trinity. In video games, players hunt for the Triforce in Legend of Zelda.

The problem with arguing using fewer than three points is that the argument may not seem strong. You risk giving the wrong idea to an audience that is conditioned to expecting three as an indicator of how complete an argument may be. It's like serving a meal with an empty spot on one part of the plate.

On the other hand, giving more than three points might feel unnecessary. Three already satisfies the audience. Rather than continuing to bring other arguments to the table, focus more on providing further detail on your existing three. If you have too many arguments, you can either prioritize and choose the three most relevant ones, or you can bucket them into three categories. Doing the latter, though, runs the risk of each point being delivered without enough detail, which can lead to questions or doubt.

Applying the Rule of Threes to professional presentation means delivering three main ideas throughout your presentation. Apart from discussing them individually in the body of your presentations, you should also list them in the introduction and conclusion (just like a five-paragraph essay) for reasons explained in the idea of Attention Span, covered previously.

Please note that there are exceptions to the Rule of Threes. The main exception comes from presentations that you have already been given a structure. For example, in an investment deck, the audience is usually looking information on (in no particular order) 1) a market overview, 2) a competitor analysis and competitive advantage, 3) total addressable market and business model, 4) financial projections, 5) go-to-market strategy, 6) the team composition, and 7) the business idea. In other words, they are looking for more than three arguments. Giving your audience what they want is more important than following the foundational ideas.

Tell a Story, Don't Give a Lecture

Unless you're in an academic setting, chances are your audience doesn't want to sit through a lecture, but they'll get excited about hearing a story. From gossip to award-winning movies to fantasy literature, stories can capture audience attention for hours, if not days.

There's nothing wrong with a lecture. Lectures often explain ideas that require the presenter to dive into a deeper level of understanding. For example, an introductory course on Python programming may require details because the audience must learn to code in order to learn Python. On the other hand, a startup pitch, for example, does not require the audience to understand all of the details of the technology (and you probably don't want to give away the secret sauce).

In a professional presentation, don't go into it with a lecture mentality; instead, think like a storyteller. There's a big difference. A storyteller doesn't need to go into all the details because a story is supposed to teach people a lesson, help them see a different perspective, convince them of an idea, etc.

There's a reason why Star Wars movies don't spend the full duration explaining the mechanical design of each levitating vehicle or why one is better than another. Based on the higher-level details of the story, the storyteller implies the idea that one vehicle is better than another, and the audience accepts it as is. Some fans may want to get into the details, but they'll go into forums or Reddit to discuss with others. Similarly, audience members can ask you questions after the presentation to get more information.

In a presentation setting, those audience members can ask you questions afterwards, or otherwise connect with you at a later point in time. Later on in this book, we'll discuss further why getting too much into the details isn't necessarily a good thing. For now, just keep in mind that it is unlikely your audience is interested in all of that. That being said, there might be situations that the details are necessary, and in those moments you shouldn't omit it.

Try It Out
Simplify the Idea

Every seemingly complex business product, technology, or idea has a simpler origin--it is answering some type of problem or need. This exercise pushes you to think about distilling the complexity into a simple sentence that explains it at a high level. It will not only train you to be more mindful of keeping ideas simpler, but it will also help you with generating main ideas or key arguments.

Using the sentence below, replace all of the underlined areas with text relevant to your topic:

A *(name of the product/technology/idea)* is a *(form it's delivered in)* that *(value that it gives to the user)* by *(how it delivers that value)*.

Some examples:

- Coffee is a drink that gives a drinker energy by providing their body with caffeine.
- A straw is a tool that helps you drink by bringing liquid from one end of the tool to your mouth when you suck on the other end.
- Microsoft Word is a software that lets you create documents on a computer by giving you a digital paper to write on.

Now, try it yourself by replacing the underlined areas with the following topics:

1. Artificial Intelligence
2. Blockchain
3. Cell phone
4. Walmart
5. Hats
6. Sushi
7. Backpack
8. Electric vehicle
9. Hammer
10. Nanobot

11. Atom
12. 3D Printer
13. Dog
14. Cat
15. Napkin
16. Paper
17. Try it on some other things you can think of. If you can't come up with anything, just look around you!

There is no right answer. You are free to focus on whatever aspect of the idea you want. For example, in my statement about coffee, I talked about the energy boost, but I could have also focused it on the taste. What you should think critically about, though, is how to keep it as simple as possible. In the straw example, my first draft might have described it in more detail (e.g., "a straw is a thin, cylindrically shaped tool…") but I simplified it by removing the description. While giving the description upfront might seem like a good idea, having too much information in one sentence can overwhelm the listener. Instead, you can supplement the description by adding an image of the straw in a drink, or describing it in more detail later.

The Evidence

An audience can listen, but it doesn't mean they'll necessarily believe. To influence that belief, you must present evidence to substantiate your arguments. Otherwise your presentation is unlikely to persuade others. When it comes to professional presentations, there are four main types of evidence you should consider when creating content to substantiate your arguments:

1. Anecdotal Evidence is a type of evidence that stems from your personal experience. It is especially powerful because not only does it provide data points that can establish more trust in your main idea, but also serves to establish more credibility for you as a presenter. It can demonstrate that you have been there, and you have done it and seen it through to success, which will give the audience more of a reason to be confident in you, and therefore, your idea(s) (Cialdini's Principle of Likeness can be found here).

2. First-hand Evidence is a type of evidence that stems from studies or observations directly related to your audience (it doesn't necessarily have to be a direct experience of the audience, but some entity the audience represents such as their company). For example, first-hand evidence in support of an HR initiative could include employee satisfaction surveys. It's a powerful type of evidence because it is immediately relevant to the audience.

3. Peer Evidence is a type of evidence that stems from the experiences of those around and relevant to the audience. People often don't like to be the first to try something--it's too risky. Showing your audience that your main idea has been accepted tells them that it is a safe bet. Similar to use of trends, other's successes is not usually a primary argument because it also lacks relevancy (e.g., just because it worked for them doesn't mean it will work for us).

4. Macro Trends Evidence is a type of evidence that stems from the higher-level patterns that exist or are emerging. A common example of this is used in investment presentations, when a decision for investing is justified by showing a projected increase in the market size in the future (among other things). This type of evidence is great to use in

support of other evidence, but is generally not the primary argument because it is not as directly relevant to the action. For example, if the AI market is expected to grow at a rapid pace, that does not justify an investment in a specific AI company, but rather, justifies looking into the AI industry in general. The presenter still must convince the investor(s) why they should be looking into investing in a specific company.

Regardless of what type(s) of evidence you decide to use, presenting the evidence is only a piece of the puzzle to convincing your audience. Thinking back to the idea of WIIFT, you must make it relevant to them. In other words, why should they care about what you just presented them? Ultimately, the WIIFT usually boils down to a couple of things: your audience will see how your main idea is more believable, or they will see how your main idea is more achievable. Those can be conditional on other factors as well, such as how they perceive your authority or credibility.

In presentations, you do not have to limit yourself to one piece of evidence per argument. Sometimes, it is better to bring in multiple pieces of evidence from different sources to demonstrate that your argument is not based on evidence that is an outlier.

In my experience, first-hand evidence has often been the most effective in convincing an audience because it is the most relatable. When convincing one of my clients, a large state-run bank in Asia, to align the incentive structure for their incubator program, the core of my argument was built around first-hand interviews with various employees handling different responsibilities in the program. The discrepancy between everyone's responses to what they defined as the goal of the program demonstrated that the team was fragmented and needed to agree on the goal before continuing, unless the program wanted to remain inefficient.

Remember the Feelings that Matter (FTM)

FTM is an idea born out of a combination of WIIFT and the UX of Storytelling. By considering the audience's experience and delivering what they are expecting, you are empathizing and better equipped to use strategies and messaging that align with the audience's feelings. Feelings That Matter asks you to actively think about your audience's feelings, because those are the ones that matter, not yours. You can feel as nervous or excited as you want, but how you make your audience feel is the deciding factor for the effectiveness of your presentation.

Just because you feel nervous, for example, doesn't necessarily mean you will seem nervous to your audience. Nervous people tend to assume their nervousness can be seen and felt by everyone in the room, but that isn't always the case. I've witnessed numerous instances where people received feedback from their colleagues or myself that didn't align with their expectations; in their minds, they imagined themselves blundering through the entire presentation out of nervousness.

In reality, they seemed pretty well-prepared, composed, and confident. While they felt nervous inside, they didn't display too many hints that implied it. The audience received a good impression and learned from the presentation.

Cialdini's Principles of Influence[10]

Robert Cialdini, a PhD in social psychology, proposed six principles that drive influence. It can be thought of as social engineering, which is the practice of making purposeful actions or expressions that nudge people in a direction you want them to go. Businesses and people use these techniques on a daily basis.

It's practiced so much that most people are unaware, sometimes on both sides: the influencer is unaware (consciously) of what he or she is doing to nudge an action from the audience, and the audience is unaware of what strategies the influencer is actually using to drive the audience's actions. While it seems obvious reading through each strategy, people forget to consciously apply them in professional communication; as a result, their communications are not optimized to persuade. Active consideration of these principles, though, will drive more success in convincing people to think or act a certain way.

1. Reciprocity: people do not like to feel like they're in debt to other people. This is why people would rather split the bill, rather than let someone else handle the entirety of it--even if they could take turns paying the bill in the future. If given something, the receiver feels more psychological pressure to return the favor. This idea extends beyond paying the bill. Imagine receiving a gift during a holiday from a person whom you did not give a gift in return. More than likely, you would feel a bit of embarrassment for not having something to give back, and might be more mindful about finding them a gift immediately or in the future.
2. Scarcity: Black Friday shopping is frantic . People line up in front of stores and pitch tents to get items before they run out. Giving a sense of scarcity evokes urgency from an audience. A fear of iPhones running out of stock during pre-orders, or new shoes flying off the shelves, or other access limitations, will influence an audience to behave in a way that increases the products' demand.
3. Authority: people listen to those they respect. Cults of personality, for example, can lead to viral and zealous followers that believe in projects

run by people like Elon Musk. Flamethrowers and electric vehicles were all invented before Elon Musk decided to pursue them, but never have they been in more demand.

4. Consistency: people want to behave in accordance with how they have behaved in the past, or the principles they want to see in themselves. Aligning with that consistency makes them feel good. This is why practicing what one preaches is such a respected action: it shows consistency in action and belief. Getting people to agree to something to even a small degree will increase their likelihood of follow-through.
5. Liking: people will do things for people they like because they want those people to like them back. A common application of this is the Halo Effect (also referred to as the Halo Error), which is a psychological phenomenon that stems from the human tendency to categorize things and an expectation of consistency (the previous principle). The Halo Effect is often triggered for attractive people; we tend to perceive them as good people in general, and as a result, they can get away with more. Regardless of whether or not you believe you are susceptible to this trap, the reality is that most of the population unconsciously does (that's my indirect way of saying that you, too, would fall for it).
6. Social Proof: akin to the idea of authority, social proof is a measurement of trustworthiness. If people see others using or approving of it, they will feel more confident in it. For example, that's what makes scaling a startup so hard: when no one knows about or uses an app, no one else cares to use it. On the other hand, network effects (hearing about it from a friend) trigger adoption at a much more rapid pace than if founders just went door to door knocking and trying to pitch a product that no one's heard about. Audiences are more likely to trust a message or idea of those around them or those they respect also believe in it.

When presenting, it's unrealistic to expect a presenter to employ all seven principles of persuasion. Keeping in mind and using at least some of the strategies outlined by Cialdini, though, will influence your ability to persuade the audience.

Dissecting the Presentation Structure

A sprinter and a mathematician are both born with the same anatomy, and it is through training that they are both able to master and perform at their best for specific tasks. The same idea applies to presentations—there's a structure to them. Once you build out a basic anatomy, you can tune for different purposes.

The skeletal structure of a presentation is simple:

1. It has an introduction that includes the main idea, and a short introduction about the presenter (if presenting to a large or new audience).
2. It contains the three arguments, each being explained in more detail within the body of the presentation.
3. Finally, in the conclusion, the main idea is restated alongside the three arguments, and a call to action is presented to give the audience actionable next steps that make the main idea feel more achievable.

INTRODUCTION	BODY	CONCLUSION
• The Main Idea	• Argument 1: Summary	• The Main Idea
• Presenter Credibility	• Argument 1: Details	• Argument 1: Summary
• Argument 1: Summary	• Argument 2: Summary	• Argument 2: Summary
• Argument 2: Summary	• Argument 2: Details	• Argument 3: Summary
• Argument 3: Summary	• Argument 3: Summary	• Call to Action
	• Argument 3: Details	

The Main Idea

The main idea is the key takeaway you want your audience to leave with in their mind. To find your main idea, you must consider the WIIFT. For example, if you are pitching a startup to venture capitalists, it may be tempting to think that the main idea of your presentation is to convince them of how awesome your startup idea is. But that's too vague and misses the point of why they're there.

For example, a primary reason for VCs to exist is often to maximize return for their investors. In that case, rather than focusing on how awesome your startup idea is, you should focus on the returns and why it is less risk investing in your startup to manifest that return. The awesomeness of your startup idea may be secondary.

The Presenter Credibility

This should be a short opportunity to help you establish your credibility to the audience. Do not waste the time speaking about irrelevant points regarding who you are—make sure that you are able to communicate why you are the person speaking about a particular idea or suggested action.

The Three Arguments

As previously mentioned, stick with the Rule of Threes in your presentation in most cases. With that in mind, a presentation should have three main arguments that support the main idea. The three main arguments should be convincing, and strategically can be considered as a one-sided or two-sided argument. The effectiveness of each type of argument changes depending on your audience's bias.

One-sided arguments focus only on your side of the picture; you give your perspective and do not put much weight on other views. This is an effective argument strategy to use when you are presenting to an audience that has no bias or favors you or your main idea. They do not have an alternative mindset that goes against your main idea; they might understand alternative arguments, but they do not necessarily agree with them. An example of this would be a protest, where all the participants are on the same side.

Two-sided arguments are effective in addressing audiences that have a negative bias towards you or your main idea. Prior to hearing your presentation, they have already accepted a different opinion that may go against yours. These audience members may bring their biases into the room. They may not want to listen; even if they listen, they may lean on their own arguments to criticize yours. Using a two-sided argument gives you an opportunity to put yourself in their shoes, and show them that you understand what their thoughts are. From there, your counter-argument can bring them to your perspective. When trying to explain a misunderstanding to an angry audience, you may want to address their side to demonstrate that you understand why they would be upset. From there, you can attempt to guide them down a path to an alternative perspective, which explains the misunderstanding and attempts to alleviate the situation.

You can use both types of arguments in combination (e.g., one-sided for the first argument, two-sided for the second one, and one-sided for the third one), or decide to just use one. There is no limitation, and the strategy is dependent on the audience you are addressing.

It's crucial to understand your audience in this case; for example, you do not want to waste time with a two-sided argument if your audience does not have any bias. Doing this may, instead, give them a different perspective to think about, and which is not what you intended. On the other hand, a negatively biased audience may think about reasons why your one-sided arguments are narrow-minded or wrong because they may not believe you understand them or their concerns (which can be addressed by a two-sided argument).

The Call to Action (CTA)[11]

A Call To Action or CTA tells your audience what they must do as a next step. You must include a CTA in your presentation. Putting it in the introduction is optional, but having it in the conclusion is a requirement. Without a CTA, regardless of how great your presentation may be, the audience will be left without proper guidance for how to act.

For example, if they agree with your internal project proposal, that's great, but what can they do? You should explicitly state that they should approve the budget for it; otherwise, they may not be clear--some may think that simply knowing is enough, while others may think that they can support in other ways that you may not need.

Sometimes, the CTA involves many next steps before the actual execution. If so, you can talk about those next steps at a high level. This will give the audience a better understanding of the next steps--giving them that understanding offers the impression that an idea is more achievable.

Part 2: The Strategy

The theories that I discussed in the previous section represent the foundation of effective, professional presentation. Keeping those ideas in mind when creating presentations will improve the impact that a presentation has on its audience. In this section, I will take the ideas I just finished discussing and apply them to the various components that make up the presentation. In other words, this section will teach you how to apply them.

Many presenters have presentation styles that have formed out of habits formed from previous presentation experiences. Some of those styles are beneficial because it helps them appear or feel more confident, connect with the audience, or inspire confidence. Other attributes of presentation styles may have manifested through habits that give the presenter comfort but may not be beneficial to the presentation; a common example is the tendency to sway back and forth when standing in place.

Some of the ideas I will discuss will be strategies you may already use when making presentations. Others may seem new or unimportant; while it may seem that way, I encourage you to keep an open mind and try it out. Let your audience decide when you practice. Your goal should be to use this section to include more effective strategies into your existing presentation style. You should also use this section to identify any current attributes of your style that may be distracting, rather than beneficial.

Structuring the Presentation: DRILS

My philosophy on structure is optimized to DRILS ideas into your audience's head. This is done by understanding the audience attention span curve, which was illustrated in the Attention Curve graph in the *Grab Their Attention* section of *The Foundations*. The graph shows how audience attention is usually peaked at the beginning of a presentation, trails off in the middle, and picks back up at the end. Therefore, we want to compress the key information from the presentation into the beginning and end, as well as explain them in more detail throughout the middle.

Direct Message Structure[12]

In most cases when you are presenting in a professional setting, the right choice is to lean on a direct message structure. Being upfront and direct shows respect for your audience's time, as opposed to stringing them along in an indirect message structure until you get to your point (by the time you get to your point, there's no guarantee they are listening anymore).

Direct message structure also takes into account the WIIFT principle discussed previously. Audiences want to align their expectations with what is being presented--once those two points are synchronized, they are more open to listening. Don't wait to do this because humans are impatient. Audiences are looking for something, and they want to find it as quickly as possible, or they'll stop paying attention. An analogy to this is page load time, where visitors are trying to find information from a website. A 2018 study published by Google cites a statistic that 53% of mobile visitors leave a page if it can't load within three seconds[13]. That's half the audience.

In my experience, presenters tend to avoid a direct message structure for three reasons: first, they think that they have to explain the backstory to justify their main message. In doing this, though, audiences don't receive a reason to pay attention to the backstory until the end. By that time, if they decide it's worth paying attention to, it's already too late.

Second, they want to seem nice. Being direct is associated with ideas of being selfish or demanding. People may assume their audience would prefer a nice person, rather than a selfish demander. As a presenter, though, being direct is one of the best things you can do for your audience. Directness reduces the amount of energy a listener must spend to try to dig out your main message.

Finally, they want to build suspense. While I applaud the effort, building suspense in a professional presentation should seldom be done. It all circles back to the audience attention curve. In the time it takes to build suspense, audience attention has dwindled. While presenters may think that suspense keeps an audience's attention, unfortunately, if they wanted it, they'd be at a movie instead.

That being said, suspense can be used to effectively strengthen a message, but try not to use it in prime real estate space; use your introduction, where you have the highest attention from your audience, to hammer your message home. That method might not have as much flair, but the message will certainly be remembered better.

- After deciding on your primary message, make sure to state it within the first minute of your presentation. It can even be in your title.
- Your primary message does not have to be specific. That's what the rest of your presentation is for. You can get into the details at a later point.
- For example, "My name is Kenny Li, and I am here to teach you about how to deliver effective presentations that can persuade your audience" can be the first thing I say to begin my presentation. The audience immediately hears what I'm here to do. I can then go into the details.

Try It Out

Get to the Point

Being direct should be simple. If you have a hard time thinking about how to state your presentation using a direct message structure, you can default to using the template below. In this exercise, we will practice with this template.

The Prompt:

I'm here to tell you about *(your main idea)*. We can achieve this through *(argument 1)*, *(argument 2)*, and *(argument 3)*.

Instructions:

1. Choose a topic you are interested in or will be presenting on.
2. Write down the main idea (refer to KISS's Try It Out exercise, *Simplify the Idea*, to help you with crafting one that is simple and understandable.
3. Keeping in mind WIIFT, write down the three key arguments as simply as possible. Your goal here isn't to provide all of the details.
4. The goal of this statement isn't to fit in as much detail as possible, it's to align your presentation with the audience's expectations. For example, you don't need to say "increase profit margins by 10% by signing a software licensing agreement with a different provider." Just say "increase profit margins."

Example:

I'm here to tell you about how we can increase profitability within the company over the next three years. We can achieve this through reducing our operating expenses, driving additional sales through a new product, and expanding to new markets.

Repeat, Repeat, Repeat

When I tell people to repeat themselves during professional presentations, they often think it's a ridiculous ask. After all, you are communicating information in a limited amount of time--redundancy just reduces the amount of time that you can get all your points across. In reality, though, you must include time for repetition; otherwise, you risk your audience only receiving partial information. Furthermore, as discussed in the Foundations section, repetition can positively influence your audience's perception of your main idea.

Think of the difference between listening to a speech and reading a book. While reading and listening both deliver information, there are features unique to each that require different approaches. For example, if you are reading a book and forget what you read a few pages back, you can flip to those previous pages and re-read it. This cannot happen with listening; if an audience member misses a point, he or she cannot re-listen to the point because you have already moved on. This is why it is very important to repeat yourself. Let me repeat that: repeat yourself.

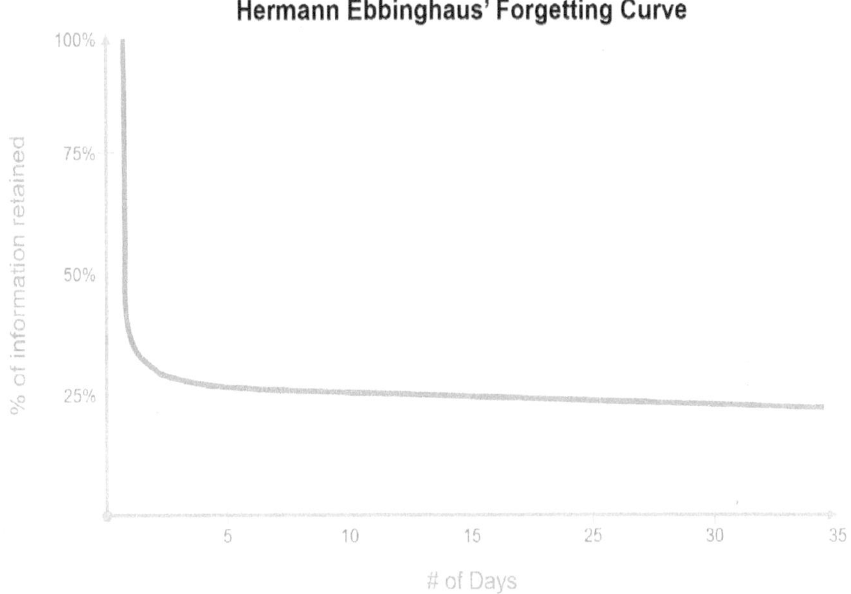

The Ebbinghaus Forgetting Curve[14] illustrates a great example of why it's important to repeat your main ideas. After absorbing new information, the experiment showed that after 20 minutes, half of that information was forgotten. By the end of the day, 70% of the information was forgotten; the forgetfulness increased to 80% by day 31. If your presentation is an hour long, then chances are by the end of your presentation, your audience already forgot much of what you said in the beginning. That's why it's important for you to repeat your points. It may seem annoying and redundant, but repetition is key for planting and retaining ideas.

The Traditional Attention Curve (described in the Foundations section under The Attention Span) is another illustration that implies the importance of repetition. The beginning and end of your presentation are two areas where the audience pays the most attention to your message. If you don't state your key arguments in both of those areas, then the audience may not hear it at all.

- After identifying your main idea and three key arguments, make sure to include them in the introduction and conclusion of your presentation.

- Don't think too hard about it; in your conclusion, you can just repeat, word for word, what you said in your introduction.
- There are strategies that you can use to reset the attention curve. With each reset, the audience's attention is unlikely to return to its original levels, but it will recapture their focus. One of these strategies is to use effective visual aids.

While repeating ideas is important, repeating keywords is also helpful to setting the tone for your audience. Keywords are words you need to decide on using prior to writing the script and designing the visual aid of your presentation. For keywords, select up to three. When selecting them, think about why you chose them; specifically, those words should be linked to some type of feeling you want to evoke from the audience. For example, if your keyword is "successful", you may want your audience to feel confident in the idea (because it can be successful).

You should make an effort to repeat keywords frequently. A good rule of thumb is to try to use at least one with each argument. The effectiveness of this practice is highlighted when you combine the idea of the Attention Span with the idea of Repetition (both are discussed in the Foundations section of this book). With a dissipating attention, a particular feeling experienced by the audience tends to disappear as well. When repeating yourself, not only do you reinforce the message, but you also bring that feeling back.

Interesting Arguments First

You might've noticed in the attention curve that while the beginning and end of each presentation are moments when the audience pays attention more, the beginning receives the most attention. That's why the strongest argument must be first. Every additional second you have risks attention loss. Giving a presentation is unlike eating a delicious meal, where someone might want to save the best for last; in the case of presentations, people would have already stopped paying attention. Remember the Attention Curve illustrated in the section, *Grab Their Attention*. Giving the strongest argument while the audience is still paying attention increases the likelihood that they will hear it, and have a better impression of your main idea.

After clearly identifying and writing down your three supporting arguments (remember the rule of threes), prioritize them. This will give you the order in which you should present each of your points. Put the strongest one first. If your first argument is weak, it can negatively impact your credibility with your audience, making it harder for you to persuade them.

- Before selecting your strongest argument, you should decide on what matters most to the audience. The strongest argument should be able to address what matters more effectively than your other arguments.
- Selecting the strongest point is subjective and can be based on different criteria. For example, if you are presenting on a topic that is already familiar to the audience, your strongest point might be something that is unfamiliar to them; otherwise, repeating a point they already know may feel like a waste of time for the audience.
- Other criteria to consider include: which argument makes the biggest impact quantitatively (effective for data-driven presentations that recommend a course of action based on data analysis), which argument is the least debatable (effective for controversial presentations that include audience members who may have a hostile mentality), or which argument demonstrates the most credibility for you and your team (effective for startup pitches or internal project pitches).

List Your Ideas

Following along with ideas is not as easy when listening to them compared to other ways of absorbing information (e.g., reading). To guide the audience, you have to do some verbal hand-holding. Doing this forces you to organize your presentation, and also gives your audience a better structure to follow along with. We've discussed some ways you can do that already, and listing every new point is also a good strategy.

Not only is it easier to follow along, but by sounding more organized, you demonstrate that you have thought about it thoroughly and also are intelligent enough to articulate it in a concise but effective manner. In other words, you demonstrate authority and confidence. Common transition phrases:

- First… Second… Third…

- First of all… Second of all… Third of all…
- First… Next… Finally…

Try It Out

List Practice

Spend a few minutes to come up with five different discussion topics you find interesting. For each of the discussion topics, write down why they are interesting. Then write down three arguments for each topic. For each of the five topics, first say what your main idea is. Start your sentence with "I want to talk to you about (topic) because (main idea)." to push yourself into a direct message structure. After this, using a list format, state each of your three arguments.

For example:

I want to talk about octopuses because I believe they are the most underestimated creatures on the planet and we can learn a lot from them. First, they have nine clusters of neurons that give each arm independent control of each other, which means they're true multitaskers. Second, they can squeeze through any cracks that their beaks can fit in, which means they are escape artists. Third, they can manipulate both the color and texture of their skin, making them masters of camouflage.

Separate the Details

Don't get into too much detail too quickly. There's a time and place for it--in the body of the presentation. By starting simple, your audience can better absorb each point you make. Eventually, though, you will want to get into more details. Providing those details usually happens when you begin the body of your presentation. In both your introduction and conclusion, avoid going into too much detail for each the arguments you list. The purpose of those sections is to give your audience a high-level understanding of your idea, not to convince them of it immediately.

Separating the details can take practice. A good way to do this is by thinking about What-How-How. What-How-How are three simple questions to ask that helps you dissect the details and separate them into different buckets that appear in the introduction, body, and/or conclusion. Here's how it works:

Imagine you are speaking with an impatient boss walking back to his desk. As they pass you, you manage to get their attention. Being the impatient boss, they ask, "What?" You now have to tell them what you want to tell them. After piquing their interest, they ask, "How?" and you proceed to explain how the idea works by listing your three main arguments. Finally, he asks "How" again, but for each argument, to make sure that each point is solid.

With an impatient person, you don't want to make the mistake of getting into the details too soon. Without knowing the full idea, they won't have a reason to listen to you talk about all the details. By first offering everything at a high level, you give them that reason.

Non-Verbal Communication: POSE

A great presenter is not only heard, but also felt. When leaders like former president Obama take the stage to speak, the audience knows to listen and trust them. Interestingly enough, a similar non-verbal confidence can be seen through the monologues of TV-show wrestlers like John Cena and Dwayne Johnson (check out this video: https://www.youtube.com/watch?v=rnNue92RSC8). A marked difference in the dramatic flair can be seen between the former president and the pro wrestlers, but both use pause, eye contact, hand gestures, and confident posture (and gait, in the case of the pro wrestler) to strengthen their points and keep the audience entertained and interested. In either case, the presenter never says, "Listen and trust me." But that's what makes non-verbal communication so powerful.

Presenters tend to take the non-verbal aspects for granted because they believe that the argument itself will speak for the quality of the presentation. In reality, every audience is a human being that has feelings and expectations that make them feel more or less comfortable with other people. While we can all act professional, those subconscious expectations aren't easy to turn off because they've been conditioned into us since we were young.

It can be cultural, which means that different people may have different expectations and feelings in response to a non-verbal cue. Giving the middle finger is a derogatory hand gesture that Western cultures use to express negative emotions toward others, but in Asia, the middle finger is often used to point out things on, say, a board.

It can also be global, which transcends geographical boundaries. For example, a smiling face means that someone is happy, and a frowning face means someone is not happy.

The POSE methodology is a framework designed to help you effectively express yourself confidently and properly with non-verbal cues. Each step focuses on a different aspect of non-verbal communication. Using each step effectively will connect you with the audience in a way that helps earn their subconscious respect, which will lead them to paying more attention to you, what you say, and also increase their tendency to agree.

Pauses Are You Friend

When presenters get nervous, they tend to rush through information. Not only does this come off as unconfident, but it also limits the audience's ability to fully absorb information. Unlike in written communication, the pace of verbal communication is dictated by the communicator. Without pause, ideas may not fully sink in before new concepts are presented; eventually, audience members become overwhelmed and may just stop paying attention.

Commonly, though, presenters feel uncomfortable with pausing. An unprepared pause gives the impression that the presenter is unprepared, consequently affecting his or her ability to project confidence and command the room. But there's a marked difference between an unprepared pause and a purposeful one.

A purposeful pause is a powerful tool for presenting. From adding emphasis to verbally separating ideas, a pause triggers various responses from the audience depending on the context.

- Using a pause in place of filler words. Filler words are commonly used when a presenter is trying to speak before the thought is fully organized. Filler words are often spoken unconsciously to fill in what a nervous presenter may perceive as uncomfortable silence. But packing in the silence with words like "uh" or "you know" only damages the polish of the presentation; using filler words frequently comes off as unprepared or unconfident in the message. Instead of using filler words, it's more effective to use a pause, collect your thoughts, and present them in a more confident manner.
- Using a pause for emphasis. Offering a moment of pause gives your audience a chance to think for themselves (think of the phrase, "let that sink in"). Audience members that weren't paying attention will notice the sudden silence and scramble to recall what you most recently said and think about why you said it. Audience members that were paying attention the whole time can use the silence to fit your most recent piece of information into the bigger picture of your presentation. In either case, you've just nudged your audience into thinking a bit harder about a piece of information, emphasizing it through the silence.
- Using a pause for transition. Along a similar concept of using pause for

emphasis, using a pause prior to transitioning to your next point lets your audience wrap up everything you spoke about previously. After doing this, they are better prepared mentally to receive your next point.

Try It Out

Jim Carrey Commencement Speech

Here's a link to the speech: https://youtu.be/V80-gPkpH6M?t=678 (the link begins the video on the part of the speech that we will be practicing. From 11:18 to 11:46 (28 seconds), he gives an inspirational lesson from his childhood memory of his father; I've transcribed it for your reference (see below). Recite the same speech with pauses in the same places he makes them. Keep practicing until you complete the transcript in the same amount of time that he did.

The Transcript:

My father could have been a great comedian but he didn't believe that that was a possibility for him, and so he made a conservative choice instead. He got a safe job as an accountant and when I was 12 years old, he was let go from that safe job. And our family had to do whatever we could to survive. I learned many great lessons from my father,not the least of which was that you can fail at what you don't want, so you might as well take a chance on doing what you love.

Observe Your Audience

You may often hear that you should make eye contact with your audience. This is partly true because acknowledging people is a powerful strategy for engagement. Eye contact with every member in the audience is not necessary--shifting eye contact across the room achieves a similar effect because audience members think you're looking at them. Locking eyes is not a necessity; in fact, even when you're talking to only one other person, locking eyes may not be necessary--just looking in the general direction is effective[15].

Often, presenters make common mistakes with eye contact in an effort to avoid gazing at the audience. Breaking that eye contact is a habit that presenters often practice to feel more comfortable in an otherwise uncomfortable setting. Some of the most common practices: .

- When speaking, the presenter starts staring at the roof or the ground. This occurs for several reasons. Sometimes, it is due to simple nervousness. Making eye-contact, especially with strangers, can be intimidating. If you do think this describes how you feel, here's a trick: you don't need to make direct eye contact, especially with larger audiences. You just need to look in their general direction, and they will think you're looking at them. In smaller group settings, doing this is trickier, but you can still get away with looking near them, instead of directly at them, depending on how far away they are situated from you. This is only a temporary solution, though. Eventually, you want to become comfortable with looking people in the eye when speaking.
- Presenters may start looking at the ground or roof because they're thinking. Usually, this happens in response to a question from the audience, but it can also occur when you lose your words in the middle of a presentation. As you try to think about where you left off, your eyes start to wander. Avoid doing this in either case, because it can give off the impression that you are trying to make things up. A confident answer should maintain eye contact.
- When using slides or some supplemental material, the presenter begins to turn his or her gaze to focus on the slides, rather than the audience. This can happen due to a lack of preparation. The presenter forgets what's on the slides or what they will say next, so they need to use the slide as a way to guide them. This is bad because it indicates that the slides are now giving the presentation, rather than the presenter. Furthermore, a presenter's eyes direct attention. If you don't believe this, think of a time when you were speaking with someone, and they started looking somewhere else instead of at you. You were probably wondering what they were looking at. In that brief moment, you were distracted. When giving a presentation, the same practice applies. The audience will follow your eyes to see what you're looking at; they'll keep getting guided back to the slides each time. They'll just start paying attention to the slides and stop paying attention to you.

Stand with Confidence

In 2012, Amy Cuddy gave a Ted Talk entitled *Your Body Language May Shape Who You Are*[16] that subsequently received over 50 million views with transcripts of the presentations translated into 51 different languages. In the presentation, she recommended doing power poses, which have been shown to increase confidence. Therefore, standing with confidence is as much about you as it is about your audience's perception of you.

Standing with confidence sets the mood of a presentation before it even begins. If you walk on stage looking at the floor with your back slouched and hands buried in your pockets, chances are the audience will wonder why you were the one sent on stage. Confidence matters because people correlate it with experience, and people like to hear from others who have experience. Whether or not the correlation is true representative of experience is another story, but that's why scammers and con artists can get away with persuading an audience.

- Don't shift weight between legs. The presenter wants to stand on one leg or the other to feel more comfortable. Over the course of the presentation, that leg gets tired and the presenter shifts his or her weight on to the other leg. This dance repeats back and forth, each time a little faster than before because the muscles get exhausted faster and faster. The hip movement might look good on the dance floor, but damages the portrayed confidence on a presentation stage.
- Don't sway back and forth. Watching you rock back and forth like a boat in treacherous waters will make your audience metaphorically seasick.
- Don't slouch. If you're an evil villain or mad scientist, go ahead and slouch, because that's the impression you want to give. Otherwise, straighten your back. Not only does it improve your posture, but it also puts you into the power pose (that Amy Cuddy talks about), which will help improve your personal confidence when presenting.

Try It Out

Professional Stance

The goal of this exercise is to help you recognize areas for improvement in your stance. Stand in front of a mirror, and talk to yourself for thirty seconds as if you were giving a presentation. You can say anything you want and it doesn't have to make sense because the content is not the point of the exercise. Instead, remain conscious about your body. Every few seconds, check your posture:

1. Is your body still straight?
2. Is your weight still evenly distributed between your legs?
3. Have you moved your hips?

Express with Gestures

Gesturing is a powerful tool used in communication that extends beyond just putting on a livelier show. It helps people remember what you said. In the 189th volume of the *Journal of Experimental Psychology*, a study[17] was examining how both children and adults recalled stories when told with and without iconic gestures. Iconic gestures are gestures that are meant to represent an idea or action (for example, if you make air scribbles with your finger to act like you're writing). The results showed that both children and adults were able to recall stories better when those stories were told with gestures. Adults were also able to recall more sentences when those sentences were expressed with accompanying gestures.

The problem with hand gestures is that, when you don't control them, the movements can indicate nervousness. Some common mistakes with hands are:

- The presenter starts fidgeting with his or her fingers.
- The presenter constantly fidgets with objects that her or she is wearing such as a ring or a cardigan or sleeves of a jacket.
- The presenter places one or both hands on his or her belly, and covers it there the entire time or the majority of the time.
- The presenter crosses his or her arms.

- The presenter places one or both hands behind him or her the entire time or a majority of the time.
- The presenter lets his or her arms hang loose when not using them, and the arms just end up flailing around.

Verbal Communication: SPEAK

Slow Down

Interestingly enough, when people get nervous, they tend to speak faster, rather than slower. On the one hand, it sounds reasonable because people want to get out of a nervous situation as quickly as possible--speaking faster gets them out of that situation faster. On the other hand, it becomes a self-fulfilling prophecy: the speaker is nervous because he or she is not a good presenter. The speaker speaks too quickly in the presentation, stumbles on words and does not give the audience a chance to absorb each point before the speaker moves on to the next one. The presentation is then a fluke and the speaker believes it is because he or she is not a good presenter. The cycle continues.

Pure memorization without the right type of practice can also result in speaking too quickly. The problem is associated with nervousness as well, but leans more on the presenter's comfort of saying everything they want to say. Whether it's about getting out of a nervous situation or trying to repeat a memorized script, speaking too quickly will 1) make the presenter seem nervous, 2) can cause the speaker to stumble on words, and 3) limit the audience's absorption of information that seems to be thrown at them all at once.

- Pausing is a good strategy for helping you slow down. When you pause, you will tend to remember to slow down; at worst, the pause will give your audience an opportunity to absorb everything you've said thus far.
- When your presentation is time-constrained (usually it is), don't try to squeeze all of your information into it. This is a mistake presenters often make because they think of information as bricks, and the more information they can lay out, the larger their wall of defense against criticism will be. That's simply not the case; instead, the audience will feel overwhelmed, likely lose pieces of information, and maybe stop paying attention overall.

Project Your Voice

Projecting your voice isn't the same as screaming. When presenting, it's about increasing your volume while maintaining a natural sound and intonation. Projecting is something you must practice, and I avoid teaching projection techniques through this book because it is most effective to find a coach that can provide feedback and personalized guidance. That being said, when practicing, it's important that you record yourself and compare how you sound as you make changes to your technique.

The first and most obvious reason for this is so the audience can hear what you're trying to tell them. Fortunately, this is not necessarily an issue depending on your setting; for larger crowds, you may be equipped with a microphone to project your voice electronically.

Emphasize Your Points

If you want your audience to remember a point, you need to give them a reason to remember it. To do that, you must guide their attention specifically to the point you are making. One way of doing this is by literally calling out your points. For example, you can preface by saying:

- This is important.
- If there's anything you take away from this presentation, it's this.
- This is a key point.
- Remember this.

You can also emphasize your points verbally by changing the way you speak. I would not recommend doing this multiple times in a single presentation because it is a bit of an act and the more you use it, the less effect it has. Eventually, it may have the opposite effect and your audience may think you're too dramatic, which may not be the impression you want to give.

A simpler alternative to changing the way you speak is to emphasize certain words. You can do this by consciously fluctuating your intonation. Take a simple sentence as an example: the dog ate my homework. Read these variations and imagine the emphasis:

- The **dog** ate my homework.
- The dog **ate** my homework.
- The dog ate **my** homework.

- The dog ate my **homework**.

While the same sentence is spoken, different points are taken away from each one. In the first sentence, the speaker wants you to understand that it was a dog that ate their homework, not some other animal. In the second sentence, the speaker is emphasizing what the dog specifically did with the homework. In the third sentence, the speaker is emphasizing that it isn't just anyone's homework, it is theirs. Finally, in the last sentence, the speaker emphasizes what was being eaten: the homework.

Try It Out

Emphasizing Words

Think about a sentence. It can be as simple as the one above.

1. Say the sentence normally. Reflecting on what you just said, write down the word you vocally emphasized the most.
2. Repeat the sentence several times. For each repetition, emphasize a different word.
3. After each repetition, write down what the implication of the sentence is based on the emphasis of that word.

Avoid Filler Words

Filler words is one of those things everyone hates but everyone tends to use as well. Common filler words include but are not limited to:

- Uh
- Um
- You know
- I mean
- So
- Like
- Right
- Basically

- Kind of
- Actually
- Really

There are many reasons why people use filler words. One reason is perceived politeness. For high-pressure communication, people frequently lean on some level of indirect structure to respond. That structure feels most comfortable in those situations because we don't want to hurt others. For example, if Skyler asked Robin on a date, but Robin wasn't romantically interested, Robin would unlikely just directly say, "No." Robin may appear inconsiderate in conversational settings.

That habit is mistakenly brought over to presenting, also. Presenters think that, if they are nicer, the audience will be kinder and maybe listen more. As a result, they lean on habits that they have used successfully in the past--one of which is the use of filler words.

The problem, though, is that people in the audience do not think the presenter is unkind. Using filler words to seem nice is unnecessary. Instead, after hearing filler words, the audience may begin to think the presenter is inexperienced, unconfident, and perhaps unsure of what they're saying. If they're unsure, it's hard to believe everything coming out of their mouth. Their credibility is affected, and without the critical piece of credibility, the quality and impact of the presentation is impacted.

Another common reason presenters use filler words is to avoid long silences. Ironically, silence is a powerful tool that builds suspense and gives the audience an opportunity to digest a message. It also gives the presenter moments to collect their own thoughts or recall the next point.

Sometimes, presenters do a good job of avoiding filler words in the presentation itself, but lean back on the habit when responding to questions from the audience. This habit may kick in because of the previously discussed reasons of politeness, but another culprit is a lack of preparation prior to providing a response. For example, it can be used to give more time to think of a word to say. The problem with doing this, though, is that using filler words as a solution is like taking a painkiller--it's not a cure, it's only a comfort. If you find yourself doing this, what you can do instead is one of these strategies:

- Paraphrase the question. Paraphrasing questions is a great habit overall as a presenter. Not only does it demonstrate that you are listening, but it also shows that you care enough about the question that you want to fully understand it before answering. It also gives other people a second chance to hear the question (maybe they didn't hear it because the question was asked too quiet, or they weren't paying attention when it was being asked). Furthermore, repeating a question back to the audience doesn't take much mental effort, and in this time, you organize your response.
- Take a pause. Embrace the awkward silence. While people don't like to entertain silence because it feels uncomfortable, a short silence is fine. To extend the silence, you can also say something along the lines of, "that's a good question, let me take a moment and think about it." After all, it's true--if it wasn't a good question that required thought, you wouldn't need to take a pause in the first place.

Try It Out

Impromptu Sprint

The goal of this exercise is to become more conscious about your use of filler words, thereby allowing you to better control and reduce their appearances in your speech.

This exercise requires you to time yourself. I also recommend you record yourself; while it's not required, it makes the exercise more effective. Before you begin the time, think about something to talk about, but you do not have to think about the points because it's an impromptu.

Instructions:

For thirty seconds (time yourself), talk as much about the topic as possible, keeping yourself conscious about moments you use filler words. In this part, recording your voice will be helpful, too, because you can use the recordings to go back and count the number of times you use filler words in 30 seconds.

Keep practicing until you can reduce the number of filler words to zero. Which each practice, try to speak about a different topic because repeating the same topic will make it easier to remember, which will naturally reduce the amount of filler words in your presentation.

Keep Words Simple

Some words are made for paper, others are made for speaking. For example, while one may choose to elucidate a complex mathematical theorem in a formal research report, speaking like that just sounds pretentious; it is more likely that you will hear someone say, "let me break it down" or "I'll explain." Even if a word like elucidate rolls off the tongue for some people, it is unlikely that the word makes a smooth landing in the entire audience's ears.

Uncommon words get picked up quickly when listening. Audience attention is impacted as they think about why the speaker used that word. Maybe the audience might wonder what the word means. Worse, they might start thinking the presenter is pretentious; giving a bad impression will impact the way the audience chooses to pay attention to the rest of the presentation.

Visual Aid Theory: SEED

In many cases, a proper presentation is paired with a visual aid--most commonly a PowerPoint presentation. This section and the next one (Visual Aid Theory: SEED) focuses on building effective visual aids that supplement a presentation, rather than distract from it.

Some advise that having fewer slides will make a PowerPoint presentation more effective. Instead, what ends up happening is a bunch of text that would otherwise be spread across 20 slides is now crammed into 10. Furthermore, regardless of the number of slides, the presentation time will still likely be fixed. Instead of focusing on slide count, focus on the design and content.

A common mistake I have seen when people are using visual aids is their depending on visual aids too much, or unknowingly driving too much attention to the visual aids. In either case, the focus becomes the presentation, not the presenter. The fact of the matter is, humans are not good at multitasking as discussed previously, and this spills into paying attention, too. Your audience will be either focused on you or your slides (if they're paying attention to your presentation), but not both at the same time.

On average, a person speaks about 130 words per minute, or a little more than 2 words per second. If an audience, which cannot multi-task as pointed out earlier, must spend 5 seconds to absorb all of the content on your slide, then they miss ten words coming out of your mouth. Because those ten words are so critical to their understanding, they've missed an important point. Without knowing the point, they can't follow along with the rest of what you're saying. Because they can't follow along, they stop paying attention. You've now lost your audience.

Therefore, it is important to use visual aids in presentations as a way to SEED your ideas. At a single glance, audiences should be able to absorb the main idea of each slide, and details in each slide should be eased in alongside your narrative.

State the Ideas Clearly

Previously, I discussed a direct message structure, which emphasized delivering your message clearly. In your visual aids, you are responsible for doing the same thing. You must control your message by clearly displaying it.

Without a clear message, you are giving your audience extra work to do. They must try to figure out your point themselves, which is both distracting and draining. Worse, they may arrive at a different conclusion.

- Your slides needs a main message in most cases. Sure, you don't have to do it for all of them (e.g., if you have a slide that's just a full-page image), but you should certainly do it for most of them and only make exceptions if truly necessary.
- A good place to put your main message is in the title because that's where your audience will go to look for it. The title of each slide is the most valuable real-estate space; don't waste it by putting in meaningless words or phrases like "Introduction."
- Keep the message short. You don't have to put all the details into the main message area, because that's what the rest of the slide space is used for. If the main message is too long, audience members may become distracted as they read through it; as a result, they'll stop paying attention to you.

Ease In the Content

Sometimes, you can't avoid a dense slide. In those cases, you need to take advantage of animations. On PowerPoint, you should be specifically using "Fade In" or "Appear" animations. When you are speaking about your first point on the slide, that should be the only point visible on the slide. After you transition to your next point, a Fade In or Appear animation should display the next point on the slide. Doing this helps your audience not only absorb information from the slides more easily, but also helps them follow along with your narrative. By doing this, an otherwise intimidating and distracting slide becomes one that is easy to understand.

- The simplest PowerPoint animations you can use to make your presentation much more effective are the "Fade" and "Appear" animations, under the Animation tab in Microsoft PowerPoint.
- For flow charts and other processes that are sequential, instead of showing it all at once, animate them in separately. This gives the

audience a visual understanding that your chart is demonstrating a process.

- Play around with animation options for a better effect. For example, the option "Start" on the right side of the top menu lets you choose whether to start the animation On Click (when you click), With Previous (starts together with the previous animation), or After Previous (starts after the previous animation finishes). The Duration option lets you control how fast or slow the animation plays out. The Delay option lets you control how long the animation should wait before playing; for example, if you selected "After Previous" and then added a 1-second delay, the animation would wait for the previous animation to finish, then wait an additional second, and then play.

Excite Your Audience

Recall the attention curve I discussed earlier in the book. Imagine resetting that attention curve with every new slide. That should be a key goal of each slide. As a visual aid, you have an opportunity to surprise your audience with interesting images, animations, and data visualizations. Don't waste that opportunity by overflowing the space repeatedly with text. Audience attention will quickly become desensitized to it, leaving you with a bored crowd much faster than if you included more variety on your slides.

- Animations and images/videos can play a large part in this reset effect. Visually, it becomes exciting for the audience when you provide them with new things to look at all the time that are appealing (i.e., not always text).
- Data visualization does not have to always happen on a graph. For example, if you want to say that 70% of users are over 35, instead of giving a simple pie chart that carves out the 70%, you can show a row of 10 people, with seven of them highlighted in a different color than the remaining three, who may be greyed out.
- For every block of text on your slide, challenge yourself to visualize it instead.

While in some situations, illustrations and animations may be inappropriate, the reality is that those situations are few and far between. Even in formal settings, the right illustrations and animations can elevate a presentation; after all, the audience is human, and open to entertainment. I have had clients who have hired me to design their PhD dissertation presentations, and I include several animations and illustrations, rather than filling the screen up with text. Usually, after the presentations, I receive messages from other PhD candidates inquiring about how to design their presentations in this unorthodox but effective manner.

Display Only Key Information

Some people have a tendency to create dense slides for various reasons. Some feel a need to pack slides with as much information as possible because it looks more intense and authoritative. Others may have trouble prioritizing or condensing key points and take the easy option of pasting everything. Some people have gotten into a habit of doing so, and don't realize what they're doing is wrong.

When it comes to slide content in a presentation, less is more. With less information to absorb from the visuals, an audience can keep more of its attention on the presenter. Also, the impact of each piece of information is better absorbed because it isn't diluted with other less important words or data.

- Keep it simple. Don't push yourself to include every detail on the slide; rather, just say the details in your verbal presentation. If all the details were already laid out in the slide deck, then no one needs you to stand up and repeat it, you could just email them the deck and tell them to email back with any questions.
- Words are not your friend. A presentation is not the time to show off your eloquent prose. Cut unnecessary words and keep the reading to a minimum; I've said it before and I'll repeat it again, don't distract your audience. Their attention is either on you or it's not. People are bad at multitasking.
- Put the most important items on the left. People read from left to right, and it's a habit that has become subconscious for visually consuming information (have you ever noticed that, on most websites you visit, their logos are on the top left?).

Part 3: The Execution

By now, you have learned about audience behavior and how it can be affected by your actions during a presentation. You have also been guided through frameworks to help you prepare the various aspects of your presentation: the structure, visual aids, non-verbal, and verbal. Everything you have learned to become a better presenter is only the first step in becoming a better presenter. The next step is to practice.

This section provides you two guides: the Presentation Planner and the Presentation Reviewer. When creating a presentation, you should use the Presentation Planner. When rehearsing your presentation, I recommend you find a listener. The listener can use the Reviewer to provide their own perspective on your presentation. Getting this perspective is important in understanding whether you were effective in delivering your intended message. You should also record yourself to observe critiques your listener provides. By seeing yourself, you will know what you did and how you can change it.

Index of Concepts

Use this section as a reminder of all of the ideas you have learned throughout the book. The list of concepts do not go into detail, but should serve to jog your memory. If you need to review, you can refer back to the section.

The Foundations:

1. The audience cannot multitask.
2. Find ways to grab their attention.
3. Ask yourself what's in it for them (WIIFT)--why are they trying to get out of listening to you?
4. Leverage Cialdini's Principles of Influence to increase persuasion.
5. Don't be afraid to repeat yourself.
6. Try to group in threes when presenting evidence or arguments.
7. Tell a story, don't get swamped in the details. You are giving a presentation, not a lecture.
8. Present evidence to increase the credibility behind your arguments.
9. How you feel doesn't matter; the feelings that matter (FTM) are your audience's feelings.
10. Remember to use the presentation structure outlined in this book.

The Strategy:

1. Use the DRILS acronym to structure your presentation
    a. Direct Message Structure - state the main idea and arguments upfront.
    b. Repeat, Repeat, Repeat - remind your audience of your main idea and arguments throughout your presentation.
    c. Interesting Arguments First - take advantage of your audience's attention span by stating the strongest arguments first.
    d. List Your Ideas - giving a list will help the audience mentally organize your arguments.

e. Separate the Details - details belong in the body, stay high-level in the introduction and conclusion.

1. For non-verbal communication, remember POSE:
   a. Pauses Are Your Friend - you should be comfortable taking pauses, don't try to fill in the silence.
   b. Observe Your Audience - eye contact will increase your audience's engagement with you.
   c. Stand with Confidence - perceived confidence will increase your audience's likelihood to listen and agree with you.
   d. Express with Gestures - the hand movements help audiences consume your message visually.
2. For verbal communication, remember SPEAK:
   a. Slow Down - if you speak too quickly when you're nervous, slow down, so your audience can understand you.
   b. Project Your Voice - no one can understand you if they don't hear you.
   c. Emphasize Your Points - put emphasis on different words to focus your audience on key ideas.
   d. Avoid Filler Words - including filler words will make you sound nervous and unprepared.
   e. Keep Words Simple - use words your audience would use, or risk losing credibility by sounding pretentious or unrelatable.
3. When designing visual aids, remember SEED:
   a. State Your Ideas Clearly - key messages should be visible on the slide.
   b. Ease in the Content - guide your audience's focus by easing in each point as you get to it, rather than putting everything on the screen at once.
   c. Excite Your Audience - use interesting animations, illustrations, and visualizations to jumpstart your audience's attention.

d. Display Only Key Information - you don’t need to put all of the details on the slide.

The Presentation Planner

The goal of using the Presentation Planner is simple: use it to map out your presentation strategically. As I mentioned previously, the key to acting natural is to have an effective strategy in place, combined with lots of practice. The Presentation Planner takes everything you previously read about into account and pushes you to consider them all when designing your presentation.

The Content

1. In one sentence, write down the key takeaway you want your audience to have after listening to your presentation. This will be your main idea.
2. Think about your arguments. Consider whether you should include one-sided and/or two-sided arguments depending on the topic. Write down every argument regarding (no more than one sentence each) why they should agree with your takeaway.
3. Prioritize those arguments, and choose only the top three. Alternatively, you can try grouping all of your arguments, and then use those groupings as arguments, but do not select more than three if you do end up with many groupings. Also, if you do use groupings, do not fall into the trap of detailing every reason within the grouping.
4. The introduction: introduce who you are (only provide information about yourself that is relevant to why you are the authority on what you are presenting), what your main idea is, and the three reasons why your audience should accept your main idea.
5. For each argument, what are the key word(s) you will use? What is your strategy for delivering that?
6. The Conclusion: restate your main idea (this can be a reiteration of what you stated in your introduction, or you can paraphrase it), and repeat the three reasons (also can be reiterated or paraphrased). State your call to action (CTA).

The Structure

1. In the introduction, do you clearly state your main idea?

2. In the introduction, do you clearly state your three arguments?
3. In the introduction, do you establish credibility to your audience?
4. For each argument, is it substantiated by some type of evidence?
5. What is the first argument, and what is the evidence that supports it? What is the WIIFT of that evidence?
6. What is the second argument, and what is the evidence that supports it? What is the WIIFT of that evidence?
7. What is the third argument, and what is the evidence that supports it? What is the WIIFT of that evidence?
8. In the conclusion, do you clearly restate your main idea?
9. In the conclusion, do you clearly restate your three arguments?

The Visuals (if applicable)

1. Make sure every slide have a concise, clear statement that explains why the slide matters. For any slides that do not have this statement, make sure you have a clear reason why.
2. What do you do visually that attempts to trigger the audience's attention in each slide?
3. Make sure that your more complex slides have animations to ease in points.

The Presentation Reviewer

When you rehearse with an audience, or even yourself (recording yourself and watching it after), it is important that the people paying attention know what to look for. Without knowing, their feedback, while it has good intentions, may be unconstructive. Therefore, here is a list of all of the points to consider when watching the presentation. You'll notice that much of it is similar to the presentation planner, which goes back to the idea of user experience. You want to make sure that your intention is manifested correctly; otherwise, you may be giving an unintentional message to your audience.

Some of these questions ask the review to rate the presentation based on a scale. Please note that these scales do not necessarily range from Bad to Good. For example, in the Verbal Communication section, when it comes to volume, the speaker can be too loud or too quiet.

Verbal Communication

1. Write down words that were spoken that resonated with you during the presentation, and give reasons why you felt that way.
2. Write down words that sounded unnatural in the presentation.
3. On a scale of 1-10 (1 being barely audible, 10 being too loud), how well could you hear the speaker's voice?
4. On a scale of 1-10 (1 being extremely slow, 10 being too fast to comprehend), how quickly was the presenter speaking?
5. On a scale of 1-10, (1 being almost every sentence, 10 being never), how often did you hear the presenter use filler words in their presentation?

Non-Verbal Communication

1. Note down any instances where you felt distracted by the presenter's movements (swaying back and forth, fidgeting with their hands, etc.).
2. Does the presenter display themselves in a manner that inspires you to trust or feel confident in their message? If not, what distracts from that confidence?

3. Did the presenter effectively use their hands for gesturing? What were their hands doing when not in use?
4. On a scale of 1-10 (1 being very noticeably nervous, 10 being very confident), how much confidence did you think the presenter had during the presentation?

Visual Aids

1. Write down words that were displayed that resonated with you during the presentation, and give reasons why you felt that way.
2. Note down any slides that took more than a few seconds of your attention at a single time.
3. Note down any slides that left you wondering why it was there (you couldn't see the main point of the slide).
4. Note down any moments when the presenter looked away from the audience and stared at the slides. Why did the presenter do this, and was it necessary?

Structure & Overall Audience Experience

Do not consider this section until you have finished listening to the entire presentation. The goal of this section is to understand how well the audience absorbed the information. Ideally, the information that the audience has absorbed is the information you, the presenter, intended to deliver.

1. What do you think the main message of the presentation was?
2. What were the key arguments that supported the main message?
3. Were you convinced of the main message? Why or why not?
4. What was your favorite part about the presentation (it can be verbal or non-verbal)?
5. What was your least favorite part about the presentation (it can be verbal or non-verbal)?
6. On a scale of 1-10 (1 being don't trust at all, 10 being trust with my life), how much did you trust the presenter as a result of the presentation?

---

[1] Christine Rosen. "The Myth of Multitasking." Issue 20, *The New Atlantis: A Journal of Technology & Society*, Spring 2008.
[2] "UK | 'Infomania' Worse than Marijuana." BBC News, BBC, 22 Apr. 2005, news.bbc.co.uk/2/hi/uk/4471607.stm.
[3] Dimitri A. Christakis, Frederick J. Zimmerman, David L. DiGiuseppe and Carolyn A. McCarty. "Early Television Exposure and Subsequent Attentional Problems in Children." Vol. 113, Issue 4, *Pediatrics: Official Journal of the American Academy of Pediatrics*, 1 Apr 2004.
[4] Consumer Insights, Microsoft Canada. "Attention Spans." Spring 2015.
[5] Posner, M. I., & Boies, S. J. (1971). Components of attention. *Psychological Review, 78*(5), 391–408. https://doi.org/10.1037/h0031333
[6] Gaddes, W. H., & Edgell, D. (1994). Learning Disabilities and Brain Function: A Neuropsychological Approach. New York: Springer-Verlag.
[7] Shalini Verma. "Presentation Skills." Development of Life Skills-II, Vikas Publishing House, 2015.
[8] Mary Munter and Lynn Hamilton. *Guide to Managerial Communication: Effective Business Writing and Speaking*; Tenth Edition. Saddle River, NJ: Prentice Hall, 2013.
[9] Stefan Schulz-Hardt, Annika Giersiepen, Andreas Mojzisch. "Preference-consistent information repetitions during discussion: Do they affect subsequent judgments and decisions?" Vol 64, *Journal of Experimental Social Psychology*, May 2016.
[10] Robert Cialdini. "Influence: Science and Practice." 5TH Edition, 2008.
[11] Eisenberg, B., *CALL TO ACTION: Secret Formulas to Improve Online Results*, Nashville, Tennessee, Thomas Nelson, 2006
[12] Bovée, Thill, and Schatzman, *Business Communication Today* 7th ed., pp. 115-16 and 408-09.
[13] Daniel An. "Find out how you stack up to new industry benchmarks for mobile page speed." *Think with Google*, 2018.
[14] "Ebbinghaus Forgetting Curve." Psychestudy, 17 Nov. 2017, www.psychestudy.com/cognitive/memory/ebbinghaus-forgetting-curve.
[15] Rogers, S., Guidetti, O., Speelman, C., Longmuir, M., Phillips, R. (2019). *Contact Is in the Eye of the Beholder: The Eye Contact Illusion.* PubMed. Perception. 2019 Mar;48(3):248-252. doi: 10.1177/0301006619827486. Epub 2019 Feb 4.
[16]

https://www.ted.com/talks/amy_cuddy_your_body_language_may_shape_wh
language=en
[17] https://www.sciencedirect.com/science/article/pii/S0022096518307136

www.ingramcontent.com/pod-product-compliance
Lightning Source LLC
LaVergne TN
LVHW090135160826
845673LV00017B/2476